W9-DIA-408

Zoo Math

The Math Zoo

Patricia Whitehouse

Heinemann Library
Chicago, Illinois

© 2002 Reed Educational & Professional Publishing
Published by Heinemann Library,
an imprint of Reed Educational & Professional Publishing,
Chicago, Illinois

Customer Service 888-454-2279
Visit our website at www.heinemannlibrary.com

All rights reserved. No part of this publication may be reproduced or transmitted in any form or by any means, electronic or mechanical, including photocopying, recording, taping, or any information storage and retrieval system, without permission in writing from the publisher.

Designed by Sue Emerson/Heinemann Library and Ginkgo Creative, Inc.
Printed and bound in the U.S.A. by Lake Book

06 05 04 03 02
10 9 8 7 6 5 4 3 2 1

Library of Congress Cataloging-in-Publication Data
Whitehouse, Patricia, 1958-
    The math zoo / Patricia Whitehouse.
        p. cm. — (Zoo math)
Includes index.
Summary: Introduces basic concepts of mathematics using zoo animals as examples.
    ISBN: 1-58810-548-2 (HC), 1-58810-756-6 (Pbk.)
    1. Mathematics—Juvenile literature. 2. Zoo animals—Juvenile literature. [1. Mathematics.
    2. Zoo animals.] I. Title.
    QA40.5 .W48 2002
    510—dc21

                                2001004903

Acknowledgments
The author and publishers are grateful to the following for permission to reproduce copyright material:
pp. 4T.L., 4B.R., 5, 8, 9, 10, 11T, 12T.L., 12R, 13T, 14, 16R Jim Schulz/Chicago Zoological Society/The Brookfield Zoo; p. 4B.L. Frans Lanting/Minden Pictures; p. 4T.R. Byron Jorjorian; pp. 6, 7 Glenn Oliver/Visuals Unlimited; pp, 11B, 19B, 20, 21 Michael Brosilow/Heinemann Library; pp. 12B.L., 13B H. Greenblatt/Chicago Zoological Society/The Brookfield Zoo; pp. 15, 17 Mike Greer/Chicago Zoological Society/The Brookfield Zoo; p. 16L Cynthia Fandl/Chicago Zoological Society/The Brookfield Zoo; pp. 18, 19T C. P. George/Visuals Unlimited.

Cover photograph by (L–R) Jim Schulz/Chicago Zoological Society/The Brookfield Zoo and Mike Greer/Chicago Zoological Society/The Brookfield Zoo

Every effort has been made to contact copyright holders of any material reproduced in this book. Any omissions will be rectified in subsequent printings if notice is given to the publisher.

Special thanks to our advisory panel for their help in the preparation of this book:

Eileen Day, Preschool Teacher
Chicago, IL

Paula Fischer, K–1 Teacher
Indianapolis, IN

Sandra Gilbert,
Library Media Specialist
Houston, TX

Angela Leeper,
Educational Consultant
North Carolina Department
of Public Instruction
Raleigh, NC

Pam McDonald, Reading Teacher
Winter Springs, FL

Melinda Murphy,
Library Media Specialist
Houston, TX

Helen Rosenberg, MLS
Chicago, IL

Anna Marie Varakin,
Reading Instructor
Western Maryland College

We would like to thank the Brookfield Zoo in Brookfield, Illinois, for reviewing this book for accuracy.

Some words are shown in bold, **like this.**
You can find them in the picture glossary on page 23.

Contents

Which Animal Eats First?

polar bear

camel

penguin

tiger

The **zookeeper** needs to feed these animals in order.

Who will be fed first?

Who will be fed last?

The **polar bear** is fed first.

The tiger is fed last.

Which Animal Comes Next?

Big elephant, little elephant.

Big elephant, little elephant.

Who comes next?

Big elephant comes next.

It makes a pattern.

Which Group Has More?

penguins

flamingos

Look at the penguins.

Look at the **flamingos.**

Which group has more?

4 > 2

There are four penguins.

There are two flamingos.

Four penguins are **more than** two flamingos.

Which Animal Eats Less?

monkey

orangutan

The monkey eats three bananas.

The **orangutan** eats five bananas.

Who eats less?

3 < 5

Three is **less than** five.

The monkey eats less.

Which Groups Are Equal?

zebras

addaxes

camels

Here are three **zebras.**

Here are five **addaxes** and three **camels.**

Which two groups are **equal?**

3 = 3

The groups of zebras and the camels are equal.

There are three animals in each group.

How Many Animals Are Awake?

Here are two lions.

One lion falls asleep.

2 - 1 = 1

How many lions are awake now?

One lion is awake.

Two lions **minus** one lion **equals** one lion.

How Many Animals Are Here Now?

Two **meerkats** stand on the rocks.

Two more meerkats join them.

How many meerkats are here now?

2 + 2 = 4

There are four meerkats on
the rocks.

Two **plus** two **equals** four.

How Can Gorillas Share?

There are two gorillas.

There is one head of lettuce.

How can the gorillas share the lettuce?

 $\frac{1}{2}$  $\frac{1}{2}$

Cut the lettuce in **half.**

Each gorilla gets half of the lettuce.

How Much Money Do You Need?

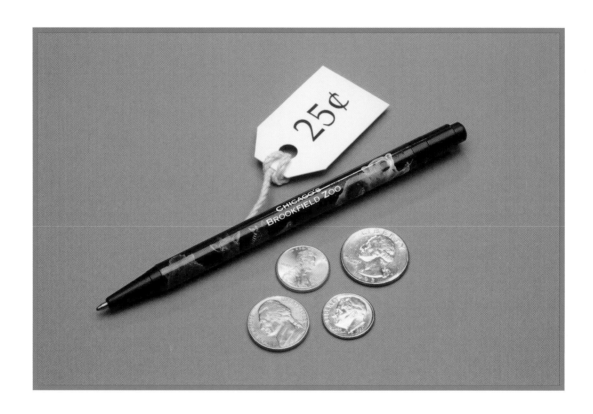

This pen costs 25 cents at the zoo store.

Which coin do you need to buy it?

The **quarter** is worth 25 cents.

You need the quarter to buy the pen.

What Will Tell You the Time?

What can tell you when it is time for lunch?

Look for the answer on page 24.

SEPTEMBER						
		1	2	3	4	5
6	7	8	9	10	11	12
13	14	15	16	17	18	19
20	21	22	23	24	25	26
27	28	29	30			

| clock | sun | calendar |

Picture Glossary

addax
page 12

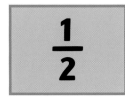

half
page 19

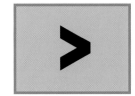

more than
page 9

quarter
page 21

camel
pages 4, 12, 13

less than
page 11

orangutan
(uh-RAN-guh-tan)
page 10

zebra
pages 12, 13

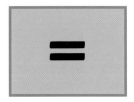

equal
pages 12–13,
15, 17

meerkat
pages 16, 17

plus
page 17

zookeeper
page 4

flamingo
pages 8, 9

minus
page 15

polar bear
page 5

Note to Parents and Teachers

This book offers opportunities for children to explore many basic math concepts. One example, found on pages 8–9, focuses on "more than." The pictures and words on these pages allow children to think about which group of animals contains more animals than another. These pages may be used as a springboard for related activities, such as asking children to recognize the same mathematical principle in other groups of objects—such as toy animals—that you arrange for them. Children can then show their understanding by creating their own toy animal groups. The goal is to help children begin to understand that the physical acts of putting things into groups, identifying sizes, recognizing similar or unequal groups, and so on, are mathematical ideas that can be expressed in words and numbers.

Index

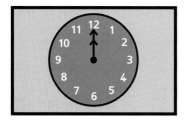

Answer to quiz on page 22
The clock shows noon. Time for lunch!